JOHN BUTTON

Exhibition and Catalogue prepared by
Robert M. Doty

with essays by
Bill Berkson and Robert Rosenblum

The Currier Gallery of Art
Manchester, New Hampshire

ISBN 0-929710-02-9
Designed by W. E. Andrews Co., Inc.
Printed by W. E. Andrews Co., Inc.
Photograph of the artist by Bob Brooks
© 1989, The Currier Gallery of Art
Cover: *Soho Sunset: Japan Orange, Ultramarine,* 1972
        Oil on canvas, 34 × 58
        Estate of the Artist, courtesy of Fischbach Gallery
All dimensions are in inches, height precedes width
14th Street: High Noon will be shown in Manchester only

The Currier Gallery of Art
Manchester, New Hampshire
October 21 – December 3, 1989

Stamford Museum and Nature Center
Stamford, Connecticut
March 29 – May 7, 1990

Rahr-West Art Museum
Manitowoc, Wisconsin
May 20 – June 24, 1990

Utah Museum of Fine Arts
The University of Utah
Salt Lake City, Utah
July 15 – October 7, 1990

PREFACE

On behalf of the trustees and staff of The Currier Gallery of Art, I wish to express our satisfaction in organizing and presenting this exhibition and catalogue. There are many people who contributed their time, knowledge and devotion to this project. In particular, I want to thank Alvin Novak, executor of the artist's estate, and Fischbach Gallery for their help and support. Many of the artist's friends have also made substantial contributions of various kinds. Planning for the exhibition began in 1986, while Robert M. Doty was director of The Currier Gallery of Art. I am grateful that he was able to not only carry on the work that he had started, but also to bring both exhibition and catalogue to their final form. During the twelve years that he has been associated with The Currier Gallery of Art, Mr. Doty has produced a number of exhibitions for artists who have made significant contributions to American art, including Edwin Sommer, Neil Welliver, Jane Freilicher, Henry Petzal, Will Barnet, Fannie Hillsmith and James Aponovich.

The trust and generosity of both the private and institutional lenders have made the exhibition a reality. Finally, we are most grateful to our colleagues at the Stamford Museum and Nature Center, the Rahr-West Art Museum and the Utah Museum of Fine Arts for hosting the exhibition in their respective cities around the country.

Marilyn.F. Hoffman
Director

ACKNOWLEDGMENTS

The work of John Button is a very intimate kind of art. He shares with the audience his special awareness and appreciation of people, moments and places. He could seize and render colors, textures and forms that were unique in time or location. His pictures maintain a balance between crisp, immaculate clarity and bright, vibrant color. He was at home in city or countryside, in New York or California. He lived in a world of physical, tangible reality from which he selected favorite images of his most exquisite perceptions. These records of his experience reveal a search for both the dramatic and the essential elements of light on the landscape.

He kept strictly to his own path and recognition came slowly. With the renewed critical and scholarly interest in realism that developed during the 1970s, he received a growing respect for his art. His pictures were included in many group exhibitions and he presented a consistent series of one-man exhibitions in New York. But, there has never been an opportunity to review a substantial body of his work. Seen together, his pictures are a remarkable visual experience which deserve a wider audience. This catalogue, and the exhibition which it accompanies, document a remarkable achievement, and a career dedicated to the creative act.

Many people have become part of this effort to enhance the recognition of John Button's role in the history of recent American art. The trust and generosity of both the private and institutional lenders have made the exhibition a reality. Larry DiCarlo and Beverly Zagor of Fischbach Gallery, which represents the estate of the artist, have been a source of constant encouragement and information. Dorothy Mayhall, Stamford Museum and Nature Center; Richard Quick, Rahr-West Art Museum; Frank Sanguinetti and Thomas V. Southam, Utah Museum of Fine Arts, have made the tour possible by agreeing to host the exhibition in their respective cities.

I am grateful to the following persons who helped to arrange the loans for the exhibition: Merrie Good, Manuel Gonzales and Katherine Gass, Chase Manhattan Bank Art Collection; Natalie Jones, American Telephone and Telegraph Company; Mary Lanier; Pat Magnani, Neuberger Museum, State University of New York at Purchase; Alleyne Miller, The Metropolitan Museum of Art; Lisa Parrott and Chuck Pittinger, J. B. Speed Art Museum; Mark Peterson, Utah Museum of Fine Arts; Cynthia Scoville, Chemical Bank; and Judith Zilczer, Hirshhorn Museum and Sculpture Garden.

Production of the catalogue benefited from the participation of Beverly K. Smith, Wells Fargo Bank; and Katherine M. Hopper, Hirshhorn Museum and Sculpture Garden, who supplied photographs. Color transparencies were made by Ben Blackwell, D. James Dee, Bill Finney, Lee Stalsworth and the firm of Plakke/Jacobs: Fine Arts Photography. Information about the artist was supplied by Nell Blaine, Helen Weaver and Jill Kornblee. Robert Brown of the Archives of American Art provided access to the correspondence. Bill Berkson and Robert Rosenblum have written essays based on their long acquaintance with the artist and his work.

The staff of The Currier Gallery of Art has been helpful in many ways. Marilyn F. Hoffman, Michael K. Komanecky, Timothy Johnson, Julie Solz and Paula Paulette have all assisted and facilitated many aspects of producing the exhibition and catalogue.

This project was conceived by Alvin Novak, a life-long friend of the artist and executor of the estate. I am most grateful for his constant participation, as well as the opportunity to work with him and the pictures under his care. The dedication and interest of Gerald Fabian have been equally important. His assistance in many ways has been invaluable, including permission to read and use the correspondence from the artist. Anne Merck-Abeles and the trustees of the Merck Family Fund made a crucial grant. We are indebted to these patrons for the enthusiasm and support which they brought to this project.

Robert M. Doty
Guest Curator

THE AMBASSADOR OF LIGHT

John Button was a Californian who made New York his home and the main subject of his paintings. The New York of his most radiant pictures is a kind of sacred grove where cornices and watertowers sprout up into grimeless and cloud-pullulating blues. Sharp New York was his cultural element — he disdained what he called the West Coast's "melancholy of hedonism," its parochial smallness — but in a sense, he never entirely left his native climate: born in San Francisco in 1929, he carried with him the bright sweeps of Northern California light and placed the integuments of his adopted city under their swayful limpidities. This temperate interloper's light makes of the high New York sky an occasion of tangible intimacy. Fittingly, Button's last show comprised views of California fields and mountains together with urban structures taken in ever-steeper perspectives from below; mounted at the Fischbach Gallery in 1980, two years before he died of a heart attack at 53, it was titled "Coast to Coast."

The bi-coastal synthesis Button managed for himself, both in and out of his art, is telling. An accomplished urban gardener (and in later life, an ardent conservationist), he tended aspidistras ("they suit my period — 1910") alongside burls of Redwoods (Sequoia sempervirens) and tomatoes in planter boxes. On his walls hung Maxfield Parrish prints and some of Rudy Burckhardt's Manhattan photographs, as well as an early 50s nonobjective drawing by Richard Diebenkorn acquired before leaving the West. There were also portfolios of antique architectural prints, picturebooks on California landmarks, histories of ancient Greece, stacks of postcards, and snapshots taken of Busby Berkeley movies on late-night TV. Of his own paintings in this small collection, *Three Serious Ladies* (1955), which he considered his first artistic success, always held a place of honor. Bequeathed to The Oakland Museum, it shows a figure group in neo-Arcadian postures before a classic, stripped-down Mission-bungalow affair with trellis and a flower border at the base of the porch. (About this simple stucco gem Button later commented: "It is the house where I was partially reared, and where I spent a year in bed with T.B. when I was four.")

In 1959, Button wrote to a friend, Gerald Fabian, about a painting by Bonnard which he had just seen at a collector's house in New York: "Everything about the painting was wonderful. What makes it good? Who knows, the incredible surface, the astonishing color, the light that pours out of it, or the feeling in it. Bonnard seems to have looked at the little breakfast table and its window, fixed his heart on all of life, and painted." A similar merger of attentiveness, technical resolve, and sentiment at once calibrated and far-reaching appears palpable in the landscapes and street scenes Button himself painted from the mid 50s on. That same contiguous "all-of-life" apprehension on his part shows up in another letter to Gerald Fabian, detailing the events of a mid-winter day near the tip of Long Island in the late 70s: "When we had left after lunch, I noticed that the fields of winter rye were a deep moss color set against a powder gray-blue of the rolling prairie. The light had been extraordinary. Everything had been extremely crisp and discrete in the clear air. The sap (or moss) green with flecks of yellow and orange, and the pale blue-gray and the azure sky . . . all completely separate as if in 'no' atmosphere at all. But now, returning at around 4:00, as the sun was going down, everything was in heavy

Three Serious Ladies, 1955
Oil on canvas, 57 x 97
The Oakland Museum, gift of the
   Estate of the Artist
(not in the exhibition)

atmosphere as the hazes arose from vast potato fields and the hollows in the woods. Deep, vivid oranges and unimaginably deep reds were set against their analogies of magenta and violet. The whole landscape was transformed again into a Romantic dream of eternity and dying." A few years previous, he had already translated such piquant observations into paint, with a series of large, vertical sunset images panning from his Prince Street loft the Soho skyline — and at one point breaking clear to a postcard-that-never-was harbor vista of the Statue of Liberty backlit against a cherry horizon.

Button was an aesthete in the strict sense of one who maintains a moral — or even religious — preference for the beautiful. His allegiance to New York was modified by an inherent civility that brought all things under a harmonizing touch. His pictures are full of smooth, if occasionally wistful, equations between natural and man-made beauty — the ultimate equalizer being light delivered through closely ordered tones. There is nothing supernatural or exaggerated in his skies, which may account for what his pianist friend Alvin Novak calls their "bright clear sadness." Bonnard, Matisse, and de Kooning were "certainly [his] ideals," while further influences — the short list would include Hopper, Fairfield Porter, Caspar David Friedrich, Balthus and Rothko, and (for clouds and other castles-in-air propensities) Maxfield Parrish — provoked intricate blends of subject and technique. The scaled-up perceptual intimacy his best paintings assert is part of what the realist wing of the New York School developed, beginning in the '50s, as a counterthrust to — as well as an absorption of — abstraction's headlong specifyings of applied paint. Beauty strikes the eye and is seized by design on the picture surface.

Much as any other contemporary realist, Button sometimes fretted lest his art "descend into genre." In fact, of all his pictures, the outright genre scenes — the Balthus-like *Fire Escape* of 1960, for instance — have the most abstract compression. Partly due to the controlled amount of incident, in his hands the condensed specifications of a pedestrian view are more likely to lean toward the emblematic. Transposed to the unruly landscape, this compositional firmness could be prodigious. Two stands of immense trees against a densely wooded hillside in *The Final Redwoods* (1975) have the Golden-Section proportions of a room by Vermeer.

Button's painting is without stunts. The clouds that bulge and quiver across his snapshot spaces achieve presence in the material world before they are recognized as effects. The clouds mass as the buildings face, in sturdy unison across the surface plane. (The frontal, shaded face of a brownstone sculpture enclosing a clock in *Grand Central,* 1965, assumes the general look of cumulus transferred to the dark zone.) The clouds are never mistaken for objects or sentimental decor; rather, they occupy the roles that figures otherwise might, with the implied motions of surrogate voluptuaries, militants, loungers. We experience them sensuously through their specific, momentary structures and their optical tangencies to the shapes of buildings, trees, hills, and other relatively stable markers along the horizons, even though the angle of appearance may leave the literal horizon below the image edge, felt but unseen.

Light is both the front and the back limit of the Button image. As far as his skies go, the light in them — Scott Burton once called it their "adagio light" — suggests and veils infinity, and naturalistically, you see the spread of light before you can trace its source. Like Friedrich with his encompassing cruci-form designs, Button fixed the transitory flashes of air and light with architec-tural solidities, as well as with the breezy candor of his brushstrokes. Sunlight and geometry cut into one another, so that the light, much as any solid factor, creates form, and with it, a complex metaphor for time.

With so much geometry to spare, Button often tucked building sequences off at the edges of his canvases, where they function like num-erals at the rim of a clock. His cityscapes break the habit of feeling one way about nature in the city and another way where nature is expected to perform as only itself: the "second nature" of the city out of doors is seen as equivalent because it absorbs, even as it derives from and frames, the primeval kind. The big difference may be in the degree of solace required when one's eyes cast about in the city's confusion and contradictory synthetic orderliness.

Button's ennobling architectural vision subsumed the disorderly and fac-titious without hiding their indignities. Responding to an appreciation of the glow in one of his more gorgeous skyward prospects, he said, "I think that particular light is smog." Nevertheless, the result of his respect for appear-ance was a kind of mathematically oriented splendor. For the viewer, the pro-jected, aimless (or exasperated?) browsing glance upward becomes a form of adoration, the exact, scintillating whites and blues pressed against bare ledges a sudden, clear-eyed hymn.

Bill Berkson

REMEMBERING JOHN BUTTON

John Button: what a flood of memories for me and for everybody who was lucky enough to know him! As I try to define him in this rush of recall, which in my case goes back to the 1960s, I begin to realize that he had a miraculously total embrace of everything you could do and be in this world, somehow juggling every contradiction. He was hilariously funny as mimic and story-teller, and often reduced us to gasps and tears; but he was also a serious, devout believer in such unfunny establishments as the Anglican Church and the Sierra Club. He could affect a feather-brained silliness worthy of Gracie Allen; but he was one of the most widely educated people I ever knew. He had an emotional chart of constant ups and downs; but he offered a haven of solid, sustained comfort to any of us who needed him at any time of day or night. He was for many of us a rock of domestic stability in his SoHo loft and California Mission Style furniture, both acquired before they became trendy; but he also wandered as far and wide as the hero of a picaresque novel. He was a friend of, and completely at home with, such famous seniors as Stephen Spender, Virgil Thomson, and Henry-Russell Hitchcock; but he gave equal social time to the young and unfamous. He was an artist whose work and temperament favored tradition and conservatism, right down to academic life-drawing classes; but he was totally open-minded and responsive to the new in contemporary art.

What an anthology of John Button stories we could all compile! Think for a minute of his travelogues. Who but John could somehow have met up with two sweet old English ladies of Victorian vintage and driven them from Paris to the remote Romanesque church of Orcival in the Auvergne, which even specialists in medieval architecture have seldom visited? Who but John, on another trip to France, could have decided to go off to the Camargue, instead of the Mediterranean, and bring back stories about the French version of cowboys and ranches? Who but John could have got a job as a tourist guide in

Africa, from which he brought back not only a wealth of botanical and zoological data but a fresh repertory of side-splitting tales about a Dantesque itinerary? (My favorite was the one about the derelict hotel run by some drugged-out British colonials who left the windows and netting in such disrepair that John and his charges were forced to endure, under the blackest African sky, the infernal alternation of 1) monstrous phototropic insects that appeared when, in fear, you turned on the single unshielded lightbulb under the torn mosquito netting and 2) the equally monstrous photophobic insects that instantly replaced these bugs from hell when, in terror, you turned the light off.)

Then there was his erudition, which flabbergasted even me, a footnote-hunting academic. He had a Quiz Kid's range of knowledge, based, I always assumed, on his Berkeley education, but constantly growing beyond the B.A. stage. (Am I right in remembering that he was the first person I knew to acquire for home use the minuscule-print version, complete with magnifying glass, of the Oxford English Dictionary?) He could tell you anything you wanted to know about anything, whether it was Greek mythology, the Christian liturgy, Japanese literature, Bach's sacred music, Finno-Ugrian languages, or the Russian Revolution; but that didn't mean he turned his back on the sciences, where he seemed no less at home, whether in geology, astronomy, or anatomy. And during the more frequent illnesses and hospitalizations that darkened his last years, he used these experiences to go on learning, ending up capable of discussing, with the specialized language and comprehension of a doctor, his own medical problems and those of the constant turnover of roommates in adjacent hospital beds.

His technical knowhow was no less all-embracing. I had a feeling that, if stranded in the California forests he fought so hard to preserve, he could have built a house from scratch. He knew all the adventurous hardships of nature, from mountain and desert to forest and ocean; and you always felt that, if by any wild chance, you were bitten by a water moccasin, John would be able to save your life with perfect timing and sangfroid. In the city, too, he was a jack of all trades, able to read legal real-estate documents that the rest of us would throw aside in bewilderment, or ready to repair instantly any major electrical fault or plumbing disaster that would turn the rest of us into a pulp. And though I can't prove it, I swear that he could not only find his way around the engine of any car or airplane, but explain its workings in proper technical language as well. His skills, moreover, were not only of the macho variety, but embraced those that used to be assigned to the gentler sex as well. When the occasion called for it, he could turn out an impeccable French dinner with no cooking short cuts, producing, for example, a perfect *blanquette de veau,* worthy of Julia Child, with a table setting to match. And if flowers had to be arranged, or identified, he was no less dependable. There seemed to be nothing he didn't know or couldn't do.

With most people, such omniscience and proficiency would be unbearable, a shield against the world. John, though, made it easier for the rest of us by his riotous sense of humor, which he used to undermine himself and anything that aspired to arrogance or propriety, and by his pervasive warmth and generosity, which always transcended the ordinary. I still remember the thrill of being paged, mid-ocean and mid-dinner, on a westbound crossing of the S.S. France, to come immediately to the ship's telephone for a call which turned out to be not a matter of life and death, as I had feared when I ran off from the table in confusion, but only dear John, telephoning from New York, to invite me, in what sounded like a gurgling, submarine voice, to dinner immediately upon my return home. And speaking of the S.S. France, I treasure, too, the memory of an eastbound crossing with John, who managed to transform our ever-growing group of hangers-on into a 1960s version of a Marx Brothers movie, with Margaret Dumont types aghast at our rowdy, giggling behavior in the dining room, the lounges, the bars, and the swimming pool. We always counted on John to shock every stuffy standard of decorum on land or sea.

Now, in 1989, John Button himself may have passed into the domain of myth and legend. To those of us who knew him, he was like some version of Halley's comet, a once-in-a-lifetime experience. But for the rest of the world, there is, happily, the enduring fact of his art, which, as a perfect complement to the fireworks brilliance of his social personality, is unsmiling, sustained, and lonely, like the art of those masters — Caspar David Friedrich and Edward Hopper — who could bring tears to John's eyes.

Robert Rosenblum

LETTERS TO GERALD FABIAN

John Button met Gerald Fabian in 1948, a chance encounter on the University campus in Berkeley, California. They continued to meet sporadically until John left San Francisco for Los Angeles, in 1952. His letters to Gerald began soon thereafter and continued until his death in 1982.

Button had the ability to write as he spoke, and the letters became a personal narrative of his thoughts and activities. His descriptions of the people he met and current events in New York have become a unique record of the artistic community during a twenty-five year period. He traveled extensively, and the letters are a chronicle of his plans and impressions. Occasionally, he wrote about his art or about the work of other artists whom he admired.

November 18, 1959   "Sometimes I think that Bonnard is the culmination of twentieth century art. I was recently taken to the house of a collector . . . over the mantle a Bonnard, certainly the finest I've seen. Everything about the painting was wonderful . . . what makes it good? Who knows. The incredible surface, the astonishing color, the light that pours out of it, or the feeling in it . . . Bonnard seems to have looked at the little breakfast table and its window, fixed his heart on all of life, and painted. He, Matisse, and de Kooning are certainly my ideals."

His obsession with architecture may be due to the fact that his father was an architect and civil engineer who built several large, commercial buildings in San Francisco. Button never lost his good feeling for that city, or for all of California, but he was just as passionate about life in New York.

April 13, 1960   ". . . a late Spring has come to Manhattan . . . in the late, heavy afternoons, . . . the great ranks of pink clouds appear to be preparing for an assumption. The endless variety of architecture in New York becomes more intimist, a lovely blue tints the city, flags curling lazily from facades; the streets are positively *enslaving*. The more tangible atmosphere that one finds so debilitating in summer seems only to imply the colossal now. Yes, I am seduced by Spring. Even as I strolled all but unconscious along Park Avenue South the other evening greeting the dwarf Yews edging a glittering yellow brick affair of the thirties and saluting the crimson and ultramarine mosaic forty stories up on an office building of uncertain period, gazing enraptured at the arches and colonnades and fantastic sculpture that spring from the tops of almost every edifice. I vowed allegiance to New York . . . no matter what."

Early in 1960, Button began to work on a painting for Gerald Fabian. He took great care with the selection of the subject, determined to find an idea which appealed to them both and would incorporate the three themes which had become the basis for all his pictures.

No date, probably Winter, 1960

"If you have any suggestions as to subject matter for the panels, don't hesitate to suggest away. Since my main concern is with the abstract and coloristic, I am not in the least rigid about subject matter . . . My thoughs have, of course, been fluttering around classical subject matter . . . a *rape* perhaps or a *judgement* of some kind. Something I trust which will leave me free to deal with nature, architecture and figures."

June 29, 1960

"Your panels are under way! and you have no idea what that means to me. I had a very hard time composing them . . . figures simply would not come, in relation to landscape. But now I have it . . . (the painting) may be regarded as the Poet Thamyris singing to the youth Hyacinthus."

July 4, 1960

"Your panels are coming along very satisfactorily. I do hope that you don't mind my messy and rather rough style. The color is rather dark, which surprises even me . . . I like to think that the painting has a kind of urbane rusticity, but I suppose my critics would be moved to hurl cries of sentimentality and primitive style, and possibly imagine that I have a certain chauvinistic attachment to Caravaggiesque subject matter when actually my greatest influence here has been Maxfield Parrish."

During the late 1950s and early 1960s, Button was showing his work in New York, but sales were few. He was well aware that abstraction was attracting most of the critical attention, but he nonetheless continued to work in a realist manner.

No date, probably Fall, 1961 "Painting goes on in New York. Motherwell's and Guston's shows were beautiful. Joan Mitchell returned from France with a show having all the freshness of action painting five years ago . . . I, of course, plod along with my figures and cityscapes, feeling about about three layers down under the surface of what is 'done.'"

No date, probably Fall, 1961 "Listen, the minute L'Aventura opens there, drop everything and fly to it . . . I'm back to painting New York buildings in deep shadow, with great banks of Cumulus rising behind them."

Button enjoyed the company of his peers and welcomed their advice and criticism. Soon after arriving in New York from California, he met a number of the painters and poets who were also starting the careers that would make them a major part of American art in the next decades. He became friends with, among others, the painters Fairfield Porter, Nell Blaine, Jane Frielicher and the poets Frank O'Hara, James Schuyler, John Ashbery.

No date, probably Fall, 1965 "I was afraid that my new picture of a warehouse silhouetted against a sky of pink cumulus was too cheap and self-indulgent, but Jimmy Schuyler said, 'you're wrong. I think it's very **strong,** and **out** and **you**.' That's what New York jargon amounts to."

He retained very clear memories of his childhood. His father died when he was quite young, and he lived with his mother, or with other members of the family. His playgrounds were the parks of San Francisco, and he also enjoyed trips with the family through Northern California.

May 7, 1966   "Memories of scenes from my third or fourth year . . . a cottage we rented on the flanks of Tamalpais when my father was first ill, and jars of 'colored water' I found in an old drawer there (it then became a favorite game to make 'colored water' by adding iodine, blueing, etc., and to peer at the world through those jars . . . I especially loved the iodine kind where the water had magic qualities of being red and green at the same time . . . and those uncut opals at the Academy of Science, displayed in glass globes, the morning sunlight streaming through windows and past the skeleton of a whale . . . an incredible blue-pink dawn at Folsom, my parents and I in a hotel room, I staring out the windows at the vast cold sky with heroic colors . . . the Berkeley Hills in Spring carpeted with poppies, lupine, indian paintbrush (my favorite because of its rich color) and the exhilarating sunny air."

Although his subject matter was very consistent, he did make changes in his painting methods. He was a good critic of his own work and was not afraid of making changes if he thought it was necessary to do so.

October 12, 1966   "My style has had a tendency to change in the last year . . . in the sense of overt and abstract geometry. The surface is much more suave and even. In fact, it has a tendency to look a bit like hard-edge-abstract painting. There is less 'atmosphere' and less romanticism. Everything is cooler and yet more overt . . . The cool, objective, and corporeal presentation of the subject is what I'm interested in. Drawing has become more crucial, color is more accurate, and composition more arbitrary. I find arbitrary composition helps a lot. It emphasizes the corporeal as part of the figure in the landscape. In any case, my new paintings are much simpler, hard-edge, and more direct."

Button liked to use photographs as source material, but essentially, his work was determined by direct contact and observation of the natural world.

No date, probably Fall, 1967

"I am a scene-painter, a buckeye, and have learned one thing. Always understand nature's colors thoroughly! Put them down as radically as you want for the 'drawing' that takes place on the canvas, BUT in the end, *suppress* the color (I don't mean 'grey' or muddy color — I simply mean suppress it slightly and it will be just right). By suppressing the colors yet retaining their clarity, you take into account the colorless *air* that surrounds everything.

In 1974, he became one of the artists selected by John Arthur to execute paintings for an exhibition sponsored by the Department of the Interior for the Bicentennial celebration. The Sequoia tree of California had been one of his great interests for many years and so it became his first choice as a subject. But the wilderness of the National Parks had already been allocated to many of the other artists on the project and he was asked to make a picture of Shasta Dam for the Bureau of Reclamation. Then his first choice was also approved and he began to work on both pictures.

No date, probably Summer, 1974

"I went to the Redwood National Park headquarters at Orick . . . The site required that I hike twelve miles into the wilderness with a forty-pound pack . . . including my paints and heavy camera equipment. I made it nicely. The trail was good and well-marked. I made it in one day. I camped-out in my sleeping bag for two nights, getting used to the absolutely primitive conditions and the wildly exaggerated size of these remote trees . . . the tallest in the world. I observed how the crowns disappeared in the early morning fog . . . three hundred and sixty feet above their bases! I wandered into the depth of this totally 'untouristic' spot observing the bases of the ancient trees, and smelling the incense of their bark. I was awakened each morning by the bellowing of Elk in their rutting-season, and watched them drinking from Redwood Creek, now shrunken into a meander of the wide, gravel creek-bed, but crystal-clear and teeming with trout. I built my fires from

Spillway: Shasta Dam, 1975
Oil on canvas, 84 x 60
Collection of Wells Fargo Bank
(not in the exhibition)

Final Redwoods, 1975
Oil on canvas, 84 x 60
Collection of Wells Fargo Bank
(not in the exhibition)

windfalls on the gravel of the creek-bed and made coffee and soup. I
watched the wild duck in flight and made friends with porcupine and rac-
coon. It was almost too beautiful to bear . . . being all alone with a part of
nature that I have loved for so long a time. I spent a day and a half in the
spot the ranger told me about. I painted seven gouaches at various times,
with various light and fog conditions. The fog lifted by ten each morning.
Sunlight . . . hot and dry, penetrated to the deepest recesses. The gigantic
trees towered above me on both sides of the gravel stream bed. An occa-
sional Laurel leant-out over the stream. Springs of crystal water burbled
on every side. The sea-breeze, unseen, whispered high up in the trees.
Osprey nested far above in dead snags, I could see them returning from
the surf with a silver fish in their talons. IT WAS WONDERFUL! But, as I
returned slowly for a solid day, not via trail, but via stream-bed with endless
fordings of the shrunken river, I began to hear the whine of chain-saws
closer and closer."

He never tired of using the buildings of New York as his subject. In 1975, he showed a group of paintings at the Kornblee Gallery in which specific references to the sites are eliminated in favor of architectonic form.

March 24, 1975

"I'm looking forward to my show. I think 'it's the most 'solid' one I've ever done, and I'm quite proud. It is consistent . . . an exploration of full-light in an urban environment and with 'no place to put your feet' . . . ie, the horizon is *below* the picture-plane in every painting. I believe that the paintings, beside their obvious 'charm', also press the limits of representation outward, toward new growth. The show represents a certain confidence in representational art and places it directly within the avant-garde, without distortion or abstraction. I even managed to paint the Empire State Building in late afternoon light, all a-glitter, and 'bring it off!' It is seen through that wonderful arcade of the building across the street. The skies tend, HEAVILY, toward the Maxfield Parrish . . . especially one of the I. M. Pei – N.Y.U. buildings with a huge, pink cumulus-bank in the sky."

July 25, 1979

"I've finally finished the 5 × 7 foot painting of the building across the street — a brick and concrete structure with Renaissance – Ionic adornments. It looks pretty good, I think. I'm starting another of a McKim, Mead and White building on Houston and Broadway. I'm using a new (to me) technique. I draw the whole thing in, in color first, using acrylic paints, so I can see right away how to make adjustments, and am also sure about all the perspective . . . Then I paint over all that with oils and much thicker and freer than previously. I find it a good way. Actually I picked it up from the British Victorian Show at the Brooklyn Museum. Lots of them did extensive underpainting, with a rather free surface. Of course, I use impasto and opaque color, which they didn't."

During the last two years of his life, he was forced to cope with heart problems, and he could no longer do large paintings. He retaliated by working with pastels, which he found easier to use and they still enabled him to make images of light and atmosphere. Although his health was failing, his fascination with the physical environment, particularly New York City, went on undiminished.

December 31, 1981 "Then, suddenly, after a dip, the road leaps high into the air on a huge causeway and all of Manhattan comes into view, broadside. It's a real rush, and probably the best view of the city. Unphotographable, since it goes from horizon to horizon. One approaches from the latitude of about 50th Street, I'd say. The air was like the purest crystal and the sun was very bright and slightly behind me. The city glittered in morning light, like some science fiction phantasm from the Victorian period. The new Citibank tower all angles and triangles. Several new hotels in silver glass. The World Trade Center like two gigantic children's playing blocks, the Empire State Building fresh and clean from the Bicentennial, its silver and red decor clear in the white light against cerulean blue. Best of all, and just peeping up over the green glass screen of the U.N. Building was the spire of the Chrysler, untarnished and glistening in its Art Deco majesty . . ."

Edited by
Robert M. Doty

Portrait of James Schuyler, 1956
Pencil on paper, 11 x 13
Estate of the Artist, courtesy of
    Fischbach Gallery

Great South Bay, 1956
Oil on canvas, 33 x 28¼
Collection of Dr. and Mrs. Richard Stern

Fire Escape, 1960
Oil on canvas, 101 x 79
Estate of the Artist, courtesy of
    Fischbach Gallery

Yellow Sunset, 1958
Oil on canvas, 40 x 50
Collection of Arthur Weinstein

Frank O'Hara and Stevie Rivers, 1960
Oil on canvas, 57½ x 76½
Collection of Nell Blaine

Thamyris at Land's End, 1960
Oil on board, 47½ x 75½
Collection of Gerald Langston Fabian
(not in the exhibition)

Coney Island, Winter, 1964
Oil on canvas, 51½ x 59¼
Collection of Harry Blumenfeld

Grand Central, 1965
Oil on canvas, 35½ x 49½
The Chase Manhattan Bank
  Art Collection

*Pavillon de Flore and the Pont Royal,
   Paris,* 1956
Gouache on paper, 9 x 11¾
Collection of Gerald Langston Fabian

Olympic Champion, 1965
Oil on canvas, 58 x 39
Estate of the Artist, courtesy of
    Fischbach Gallery

Ca d'Oro, Venice, 1966
Gouache on paper, 10 x 12
Collection of Dr. and Mrs. Leonard
  Kornblee

Canadian Street, 1968
Oil on canvas, 52 x 84
Hirshhorn Museum and Sculpture
   Garden, Smithsonian Institution,
   The Joseph H,. Hirshhorn
   Bequest, 1981

Swarthmore, 1970
Gouache on paper, 9 x 12
Hirshhorn Museum and Sculpture
    Garden, Smithsonian Institution,
    The Joseph H. Hirshhorn
    Bequest, 1981

Philadelphia, 1970
Gouache on paper, 9 x 12
Hirshhorn Museum and Sculpture
  Garden, Smithsonian Institution,
  The Joseph H. Hirshhorn
  Bequest, 1981

After David, 1972
Gouache on paper, 15¾ x 11¾
Collection of Dr. and Mrs. Richard Stern

Sunset No. 1, 1972
Oil on canvas, 38 x 52
Hirshhorn Museum and Sculpture
  Garden, Smithsonian Institution,
  The Joseph H. Hirshhorn
  Bequest, 1981

Surfer, 1972
Gouache on paper, 12 x 16
Collection of Gerald Langston Fabian

Boy in Army Coat, 1972
Gouache on paper, 16 x 12
Estate of the Artist, courtesy of
    Fischbach Gallery

Charles Ludlam as Bluebeard, 1972
Gouache on paper, 16 x 12
Estate of the Artist, courtesy of
   Fischbach Gallery

Prince Street, 1972
Gouache on paper, 11⅝ x 15⅜
The Currier Gallery of Art,
  gift of A. Aladar Marberger

Soho Sunset: Chrome and Rose, 1973
Oil on canvas, 58 x 32
Collection of the Metropolitan Life
    Insurance Company

Soho Sunset: Coral and Black, 1973
Oil on canvas, 36 x 60
Estate of the Artist, courtesy of
   Fischbach Gallery

Rooftops: Skylight, 1975
Oil on canvas, 30 x 40
Fischbach Gallery

Field Study II: Final Redwoods, 1974
Gouache on paper, 29¾ x 23¾
Collection of Henry Heuser

Rooftops: White Water Tower, 1975
Oil on canvas, 30 x 40
American Telephone & Telegraph
  Company

Rooftops: Red Warehouse, 1975
Oil on canvas, 38 x 52
Utah Museum of Fine Arts, University of
　Utah, purchased with funds from the
　Charles E. Merrill Trust and the
　National Endowment for the Arts

Field Study for Spillway, Shasta Dam II,
  1974
Gouache on paper, 19¾ x 15¾
Estate of A. Aladar Marberger

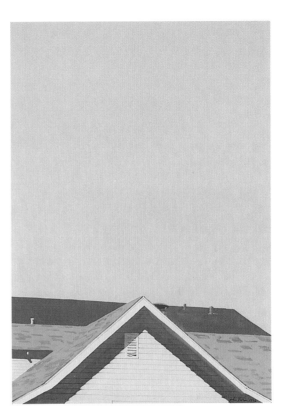

*Diptych with Palm Tree, Hollywood,
California,* 1976
Gouache on paper, 20 x 14⅛, each
Neuberger Museum, State University of
New York at Purchase, gift of Martin
J. Sklar

Stucco Bungalow, 1976
Gouache on paper, 14 x 20
Rahr-West Art Museum

Lake Wesserunset: Sunset, 1977
Gouache on paper, 19¾ x 25¾
Collection of Dr. and Mrs. James A.
   Slater

Twenty-third Street: High Noon, 1978
Gouache on paper, 19¾ x 26¾
Collection of the Chemical Bank

14th Street: High Noon, 1977
Gouache on paper, 19¾ x 25¾
The Metropolitan Museum of Art, gift of
   Dr. and Mrs. Robert Carroll

Sunday Morning, 1980
Oil on canvas, 60 x 84
Estate of the Artist, courtesy of
    Fischbach Gallery

Coast Range Hills: Homage to Gottardo
   Piazzoni, 1982
Oil on canvas, 36 x 96
Collection of Gerald Langston Fabian

Watertower, Morning, 1982
Pastel on paper, 6 x 9
Estate of the Artist, courtesy
   Fischbach Gallery

Columbia Presbyterian III, 1982
Pastel on paper, 9½ x 12¼
Estate of the Artist, courtesy of
   Fischbach Gallery

On Noyac Path, 1982
Gouache on paper, 20¾ x 17
Estate of the Artist, courtesy of
  Fischbach Gallery

Autumn Scene (Blue-Grey Sky), 1982
Watercolor on paper, 18 x 21
Estate of the Artist, courtesy of
   Fischbach Gallery

BIOGRAPHY

1929　Born in San Francisco
1982　Died in New York

EDUCATION

1947-48　Studies at University of California, Berkeley
1949-51　Studies at California School of Fine Arts and University of California Medical Center, San Francisco
1951-52　Studies with Howard Warshaw and Altina Barrett, Beverly Hills, California
1953　Studies at Hans Hofmann School of Fine Arts, New York
1964　Studies with Willard Cummings, New York

TEACHING POSITIONS

1964-65　Skowhegan School of Painting and Sculpture, Skowhegan, Maine
1965-66　School of Visual Arts, New York
1967-68　College of Art, Architecture & Planning, Cornell University, Ithaca, New York
1968-82　School of Visual Arts, New York
1969-70　Swarthmore College, Swarthmore, Pennsylvania
1975-82　Graduate School of Fine Arts, University of Pennsylvania, Philadelphia
1975　Maryland Institute of Art, Baltimore

COMMISSION

1972　Mural for The Firehouse, (with Mario Dubsky), Gay Activists Alliance, New York

AWARDS

1952　Prize, Los Angeles County Museum, Los Angeles, California
1961　Ingram Merrill Foundation Grant, also 1969, 1974 and 1982
1964　Prize, Silvermine Guild of Artists, Norwalk, Connecticut

ONE-MAN EXHIBITIONS

1957   Tibor de Nagy Gallery, New York

1963-76   Kornblee Gallery, New York

1967   Franklin Siden Gallery, Detroit, Michigan

1969   Wilcox Gallery, Swarthmore College, Swarthmore, Pennsylvania

1970   The J. L. Hudson Gallery, Troy, Michigan

1978   Fischbach Gallery, New York

1978   Gallery of July & August, Woodstock, New York

1980   Fischbach Gallery, New York

1984   "John Button: An American Painter," The College Gallery, Kean College, Union, New Jersey

           "John Button: Paintings and Gouaches," Visual Arts Museum, School of Visual Arts, New York

1986   "John Button: The Last Works," Fischbach Gallery, New York

1990   Fischbach Gallery, New York

GROUP EXHIBITIONS

1952   "Annual Exhibition: Artists of Los Angeles and Vicinity," Los Angeles County Museum, Los Angeles, California

1953   "Annual Exhibition: Artists of Los Angeles and Vicinity," Los Angeles County Museum, Los Angeles, California

1954   "Stable Annual," Stable Gallery, New York

1955   "Stable Annual," Stable Gallery, New York

1956   "Three Painters Introduced by Three Poets," Tibor de Nagy Gallery, New York

1959   "Gallery Group," Tanager Gallery, New York

1960   "Gallery Group," Tanager Gallery, New York

1960   "Appearance and Reality," David Herbert Gallery, New York

1961   "The Figure in Contemporary Art," American Federation of Arts, New York and tour

1962   "Art Lending Service," The Museum of Modern Art, New York

           "The Continuing Tradition of Realism in American Art," Hirschl and Adler Gallery, New York

"Figures," Kornblee Gallery, New York

"Recent Painting USA: The Figure," The Museum of Modern Art, New York and tour

"Gallery Group," Tanager Gallery, New York

"Art in Embassies," The Museum of Modern Art, New York, tour

1963 "Landscape in Recent American Painting," The Art Center, New School for Social Research, New York

"Recent Landscapes by Eight Americans," The Museum of Modern Art, New York, tour

1965 "Eight Landscape Painters," The International Council, The Museum of Modern Art, New York, Palazzo Collicola, Spoleto, Italy, tour

1968 "Realism Now," Vassar College Art Gallery, Poughkeepsie, New York

1969 "Contemporary Portraits," The Museum of Modern Art, New York, tour

1970 "Painterly Realism," American Federation of Arts, New York and tour

"Painting and Sculpture Today," Indianapolis Museum of Art, Indianapolis, Indiana

"The Representational Spirit," University Art Gallery, State University of New York at Albany

1972 "The American Landscape," Art Gallery, School of Fine and Applied Arts, Boston University, Boston, Massachusetts

"Viewpoints 7: Painters of the Land and Sky," The Picker Gallery, Dana Arts Center, Colgate University, Hamilton, New York

1973 "The Male Nude," Emily Lowe Gallery, Hofstra University, Hempstead, New York

"A Sense of Place," Joslyn Art Museum, Omaha, Nebraska and tour

1974 "Painting and Sculpture Today," Indianapolis Museum of Art, Indianapolis, Indiana

1976 "Three Centuries of the American Nude," The New York Cultural Center

1976 "America 1976," Department of the Interior at the Corcoran Gallery of Art, Washington, DC

"A Selection of American Art: The Skowhegan School 1946-1976,"
Institute of Contemporary Art, Boston, Massachusetts

1977 "Artist's Choice: Figurative Art in New York: Contemporary Watercolors and Pastels," Art Museum, Indiana University, Bloomington
"Artists Salute Skowhegan," Kennedy Galleries, Inc., New York

1978 "American Realism," College of William and Mary, Williamsburg, Virginia
"Painterly Realism," Watson/de Nagy & Company, Houston, Texas
"Survey of Realism," Sardoni Art Gallery, Wilkes College, Wilkes-Barre, Pennsylvania

1979 "New York Now," Phoenix Art Museum, Arizona
"Painterly Realism in America," A.J. Wood Gallery, Philadelphia, Pennsylvania
"16 Realists: A Selection," Art Gallery, Horace Mann School, Bronx, New York
"Selections from Skowhegan," The Art Gallery of the University of Maryland, College Park
"Summertime," Droll / Kolbert Gallery, New York
"The Urban Landscape," Wave Hill, Bronx, New York

1980 "Art from Houston Corporations 1," Sewall Art Gallery, Rice University, Houston, Texas
"Contemporary Naturalism: Works of 1970s," Nassau County Museum of Fine Art, Roslyn Harbor, New York
"Photo-Realism," Jeffrey Fuller Fine Art at the Kron Collection, Philadelphia, Pennsylvania
"Realism Photo-Realism," Philbrook Art Center, Tulsa, Oklahoma
"Selections from the Fischbach Gallery," State University of New York at Cortland

1982 "An Appreciation of Realism," Museum of Art, Munson-Williams-Proctor Institute, Utica, New York
"Cloudworks," Stuart Neill Gallery, New York
"Contemporary Realist Painting: A Selection," Museum of Fine Arts, Boston, Massachusetts

1983   "In Honor of the Brooklyn Bridge," David Finlay, Jr. Contemporary, New York
"Works of the Faculty and Students of the Department of Fine Arts," University
of Pennsylvania, Philadelphia

1984   "Art and Friendship: A Tribute to Fairfield Porter," Guild Hall Museum,
East Hampton, New York
"Drawings by 77," Forum Gallery, New York
"Landscape," Matthews Hamilton Gallery, Philadelphia, Pennsylvania

1985   "American Realism," William Sawyer Gallery, San Francisco, California
"The Artist Celebrates New York: Selected Paintings from the Metropolitan
Museum of Art," Bronx Museum of the Arts, New York and tour
"American Realism: Twentieth Century Drawings and Watercolors from the
Glenn C. Janss Collection," San Francisco Museum of Modern Art,
San Francisco, California and tour
"City Views: Panoramas to Particulars," CIGNA Museum and Art Collection,
Philadelphia, Pennsylvania
"The Gathering of the Avant-garde," Kenkeleba House, New York

1986   "American Cityscape," Frank Bernarducci Gallery, New York
"Mainly on the Plane," 56 Bleecker Gallery, Ltd., New York

1988   "Contemporary Nudes," Contemporary Art at One Penn Plaza, New York
"Memorial for John Bernard Myers," Kouras Gallery, New York

BIBLIOGRAPHY

STATEMENTS AND WRITINGS BY THE ARTIST

Katz, Paul and Jackson, Ward, eds.: *Art Now: New York* 1:1 June 1969

"Frank's Grace" *Panjandrum* Nos. 2-3 San Francisco, California, 1973

Fag Rag p. 15 New York Summer 1974

"Willard Warren Cummings: A Tribute" (Eulogy delivered at the South Solon Meeting House, Maine, July 27, 1975) privately printed

BOOKS AND EXHIBITION CATALOGUES

Arthur, John: *Realist Drawings and Watercolors: Contemporary Works on Paper* New York Graphic Society, Boston 1980

Berkson, Bill, ed.: *In Memory of My Feelings: A Selection of Poems by Frank O'Hara* The Museum of Modern Art, New York 1967

Berkson, Bill and Le Suer, Joe, eds.: *Homage to Frank O'Hara* Big Sky, Bolinas, California, 1978

Cohan, Zara: *John Button: An American Painter* The College Gallery, Kean College, Union, New Jersey, 1984

Downes, Rackstraw: *Fairfield Porter: Art In Its Own Terms: Selected Criticism 1935-1975* Taplinger Publishing Co., New York 1979

Finch, Christopher: *American Watercolors* Abbeville Press, New York 1986

Goodyear, Frank H., Jr.: *Contemporary American Realism Since 1960* New York Graphic Society in association with the Pennsylvania Academy of the Fine Arts, Boston and Philadelphia 1981

Gussow, Alan: *A Sense of Place: The Artist and the American Land* Friends of the Earth, San Francisco, California, 1971

Martin, Alvin: *American Realism: Twentieth Century Drawings and Watercolors from the Glenn C. Janss Collection* Harry N. Abrams, Inc. in association with the San Francisco Museum of Modern Art, New York 1985

Pisano, Ronald: *Long Island Landscape Painting in the Twentieth Century* Little, Brown and Co., Boston 1990

Rosenblum, Robert: *Modern Painting and the Northern Romantic Tradition: Friedrich to Rothko* Harper and Row, New York 1975

Severinghaus, Walter J., ed.: *Art at Work: The Chase Manhattan Collection* E. P. Dutton, Inc., New York 1984

PERIODICALS AND NEWSPAPERS

Ashbery, John: "1976 And All That" *New York Magazine* April 3, 1978

Ashton, Dore: "What About the Human Figure?" *The Studio* 164:68-71 August 1962

Author unknown: "Obituary" *Art in America* 71:168 February 1983

Berkson, Bill: "Art Chronicle" *Kulchur* 2:38-39 Autumn 1962

——: "Reviews and Previews: John Button" *Art News* 61:48 February 1963

Brenson, Michael: "John Button Dies: Cityscape Painter" *The New York Times,* December 15, 1982

Burton, Scott: "John Button" *Art and Literature* No. 11: 69-81 Winter 1967

——: "Reviews and Previews: John Button" *Art News* 67:8-9 October 1968

Campbell, Lawrence: "Reviews and Previews: John Button" *Art News* 69:12 December 1970

Davis, James: "Hard Shapes, Simple Themes Highlight Button's Exhibition" *The Swarthmore College Phoenix* 90:3 October 3, 1969

Derfner, Phyllis: "New York" *Art International* 18:19-20 January 1974

Dlugas, Tim: "Figure into Fantasy: The Erotic in John Button's Drawings of Male Nudes" *ACM The Journal of the Artist's Choice Museum* 4:20-21 Spring-Summer 1985

Ellenzweig, Allen: "Reviews: John Button" *Arts Magazine* 49:4 May 1975

——: "John Button and Romantic Reality" *Arts Magazine* 50:92-94 November 1975

——: "Reviews: John Button" *Arts Magazine* 51:27 September 1976

Frank, Peter: "New York Reviews: John Button" *Art News* 77:174 September 1978

Glueck, Grace: "John Button" *The New York Times* April 6, 1984

Gruen, John: "Friday Tour of Art: John Button" *World Journal Tribune,* April 14, 1967

——: "Art in New York: John Button" *New York Magazine* October 11, 1968

Henry, Gerrit: "Reviews and Previews: John Button" *Art News* 71:14-15 Summer 1972

——: "Painterly Realism and the Modern Landscape" *Art in America* 69:112-119 September 1981

——: "John Button at Fischbach" *Art in America* 74:136-137 December 1986

Hughes, Robert: "Face of the Land" *Time* 108:78-80 July 5, 1976

Kozloff, Max: "New York Letter" *Art International* 6:36 September 1962

Kramer, Hilton: "John Button" *The New York Times* April 8, 1967

——: "Poetry Drawn from the Ordinary" *The New York Times* September 28, 1968

——: "An Art of Conservation" *The New York Times* February 9, 1969

——: "Art: Landscapes of Button and Cohen" *The New York Times* March 7, 1970

——: "John Button" *The New York Times* April 5, 1975

——: "John Button" *The New York Times,* June 4, 1976

Kuspit, Donald B., ed.: "New York Today: Some Artists Comment" *Art in America* 65:78-85 September 1977

Larson, Kay: "Painting the Public Lands" *Art News* 75:32-36 January 1976

Little, Carl: "The Brooklyn Bridge" *Arts Magazine* 57:7 June 1983

Lubell, Ellen: "Reviews: John Button" *Arts Magazine* 46:60-61 Summer 1972

Nemser, Cindy: "The Male Nude Arrives at Last" *Changes* 14-15 July 1972

Perl, Jed: "The Vertical Landscape: 'In the Redwood Forest Dense' " *Art in America* 64:59-63 January 1976

Petersen, Valerie: "U.S. Figure Painting: Continuity and Cliché" *Art News* 61:36-38,51 Summer 1962

Raynor, Vivien: "Lois Dodd — John Button" *The New York Times* April 7, 1978

——: "John Button" *The New York Times* September 26, 1986

Romagnoli, Robert: "John Button: New York from Aloft" *Strata* (School of Visual Arts) 15, 1975

Rosenblum, Robert: "Painting America First" *Art in America* 64:82-85 January 1976

Russell, John: "The Many Faces of Naturalism" *The New York Times* August 10, 1980

Sandler, Shirley: "John Button" *SVA Alumni Journal 1983* 16-17 School of Visual Arts Press, 1983

Saslow, James M.: "Obituary" *The Advocate,* Issue 362 March 3, 1983

Schuyler, James: "Reviews and Previews: Three Painters" *Art News* 55:8 October 1956

——: "Review of Exhibitions: John Button at Kornblee" *Art in America* 63:100-101 September 1975

Shirey, David L.: "Male Nudes in Art Shown" *The New York Times* December 2, 1973

Tillim, Sidney: "Month in Review" *Arts Magazine* 37:46-49 April 1963

Wasserman, Emily: "New York" *Artform* 7:59 December 1968

Weaver, Helen: "Button in New York City" *Woodstock Times* November 21, 1973

Welish, Marjorie: "Reviews: John Button and Lois Dodd at Fischbach" *Art in America* 66:128 September 1978

Yourgrau, Barry: "John Button" *Arts Magazine* 55:35 September 1980

TELEVISION

"Art and Artists from the Video Data Bank" The School of the Art Institute of Chicago, 1980

COLLECTIONS

INSTITUTIONS

Boise Art Museum, Idaho
Columbia University, New York, New York
The Currier Gallery of Art, Manchester, New Hampshire
The Grey Art Gallery and Study Center, New York University Art
  Collection, New York
Hirshhorn Museum and Sculpture Garden, Smithsonian Institution,
  Washington, DC
The Metropolitan Museum of Art, New York, New York
The Museum of Modern Art, New York, New York
Neuberger Museum, State University of New York at Purchase
The Newark Museum, New Jersey
The Oakland Museum, California
Palm Springs Desert Museum, Inc., California
The Parrish Art Museum, Southampton, New York
The Port Authority of New York and New Jersey, New York
Portland Museum of Art, Maine
Rahr-West Art Museum, Manitowoc, Wisconsin
Utah Museum of Fine Arts, University of Utah, Salt Lake City
Wadsworth Atheneum, Hartford, Connecticut
Weatherspoon Art Gallery, University of North Carolina at Greensboro

CORPORATIONS

Amerada Hess Corporation, New York, New York
American Telephone and Telegraph Company, New York, New York
Becton, Dickinson and Company, Franklin Lakes, New Jersey
195 Broadway Corporation, New York, New York
Brunswick Corporation, Skokie, Illinois
Chase Manhattan Bank, N.A., New York, New York
Chemical Bank, New York, New York
Chicopee, New Brunswick, New Jersey
Commerce Bancshares, Inc., Kansas City, Missouri
CIGNA Service Company, Philadelphia, Pennsylvania
Estee Lauder Corporation, New York, New York
Lewco Securities Corporation, New York, New York
Metropolitan Life Insurance Company, New York, New York
Milbank, Tweed, Hadley & McCloy, New York, New York
Prudential Insurance Company of America, Newark, New Jersey
RJR Nabisco, Inc., Atlanta, Georgia
Shearson, Lehman, Hutton, Inc., New York, New York
Simpson, Thacher & Bartlett, New York, New York
Sondita Enterprises, Inc., Tucson, Arizona
Wellington Management Corporation, Boston, Massachusetts
Wells Fargo Bank, N.A., San Francisco, California